Read Write

Supporti
child's phonics
learning at home

Parent
Handbook

Ruth Miskin and Mitch Cronick

OXFORD
UNIVERSITY PRESS

Contents

Dear Parent/Guardian

While I was a headteacher in London I began to devise a programme that would get all children to read and write quickly and easily. The programme has now been widely used, tested and developed and the result is *Read Write Inc. Phonics*.

Following the huge success of *Read Write Inc. Phonics* in schools, and many parental requests, I have created this kit, which includes this Parent Handbook, Flashcards, a Handwriting Workbook and other resources to support your child to learn to read at home.

At the core of *Read Write Inc. Phonics* is the systematic teaching of all the common sounds in the English language. Children are taught to recognise the sounds and to put them together, to 'sound-blend' them, into words for reading.

First you need to help your child learn the sounds on the Flashcards. Once your child has done this, they can begin to sound-blend to read words. Your child can then move on to writing the letters that make the sounds and begin to spell words.

If you follow the step-by-step guidance given in this Parent Handbook, and on the parent tutorial videos online at **www.ruthmiskin.com** or **www.oxfordowl.co.uk/for-home**, you will be giving your child the best possible support. Day by day, you will see your child's confidence grow – and there are few things more rewarding than seeing your child learn to read.

Best wishes,

Ruth Miskin

Introduction

This Handbook will give you detailed, easy-to-follow advice on using the **Flashcards, Handwriting Workbook** and other resources in *My Reading & Writing Kit* to support your child at every stage.

By following the activities in this book, you can help your child to learn the Speed Sounds, blend sounds to make words, write the letters and spell words.

The other resources provided in the kit are:

Flashcards

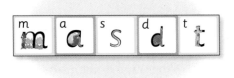

Bedroom Frieze

Wipe-clean Sheet and Pen

Handwriting Workbook

★ First, read the instructions on the **Flashcards** to help your child to read the Speed Sounds. Teach your child the sounds in the order on the **Flashcards** and remember to use the sound, not the letter name, so *a* as in *apple*, not *ay*.

★ As your child learns to read the sounds, follow the plans on pages 12–14 to help them to write the sounds.

★ Once your child has learnt to blend the first group of sounds (*m*, *a*, *s*, *d*, *t*), follow the plans on pages 15–21 to help your child to blend the sounds together to read words.

★ Guidance on pages 22–23 will help you to support your child to spell the words in the sound-blending activities.

Pure sounds

When teaching your child the Speed Sounds, it's very important that you don't add an intrusive *uh* to the end of consonant sounds. Try to pronounce them as 'pure' sounds: *m* not *muh*, *f* not *fuh*, *l* not *luh*, etc. This takes some practice, but if your child learns to pronounce the sounds as pure sounds they will find it easier later to put the sounds together to make a word. For example, it is easier to put the sounds *c-a-t* together than *cuh-a-tuh*. (A slight *uh* cannot be helped when saying *b*, *d*, *g*, *j*, *w* and *y*.)

Stretchy and bouncy sounds

As you start to teach your child the first group of sounds on the **Flashcards**, you will notice that each sound is either 'stretchy' or 'bouncy'. The following pages provide guidance on how to teach the stretchy sounds (pages 6–7) and bouncy sounds (pages 8–9).

For an introduction to *Read Write Inc. Phonics*, videos and more, go to **www.oxfordowl.co.uk/for-home**

Reading the stretchy sounds with your child

You will teach your child the Speed Sounds in groups, starting with *m*, *a*, *s*, *d*, *t* (see the **Flashcards** instructions). The colour strip at the top of each **Flashcard** shows the group each sound belongs to. Use the plan below to help your child read each stretchy sound, e.g. *m*. The stretchy sounds are

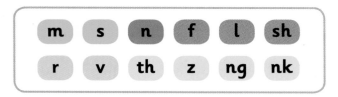

Using the Flashcards

Start by holding up the **Flashcard** for *m* (letter side). Stretch **mmmmmm** as you press your lips together hard.

Read the sound

1   Copy a simple version of Maisie and the mountains on to a piece of paper. Run your finger down Maisie and then over the two mountains, saying **mmmmmm**. Say **mountain** as you reach the end of the second mountain. Ask your child to repeat.

2 Write **m** on the paper beside your copy of Maisie and the mountains. Make it the same size. Run your finger down and then over **m**, saying **mmmmmm**. Say **m** just as you reach the end of **m**. Ask your child to repeat. Repeat Steps 1 and 2 a few times.

3 Explain that the **Flashcard** (picture side) is the same as your drawing. Tell your child that the letter is hidden behind the picture. Show the letter side. Say **m**.

4 Ask your child to say **m** or **mountain** as you flip the card a few times.

Review the sounds

Once you have a number of sounds to review, hide the new sound in the pack of sounds taught so far. Ask your child to read the sounds (without bouncing or stretching them) and spot the new sound. Increase the speed as your child gains confidence.

Use the **Bedroom Frieze** to review the sounds taught so far and any new sounds every evening. Point to the sounds your child has learnt in and out of order. Increase the speed as your child gains confidence.

Reading the bouncy sounds with your child

Use this plan to help your child read each bouncy sound, e.g. **_a_**. The bouncy sounds are

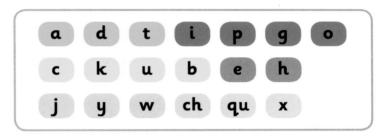

Using the Flashcards

Start by holding up the **Flashcard** for **_a_** (letter side). Bounce **a-a-a-a-a-a**. Open your mouth wide, as if to take a big bite of an apple.

Read the sound

1   Copy a simple version of the apple on to a piece of paper. Run your finger round the apple, saying **a-a-a-a-a-a**. Say **apple** as you reach the end of the apple. Ask your child to repeat.

2   Write **a** on the paper beside your copy of the apple. Make it the same size. Run your finger round the **a**, saying **a-a-a-a-a-a**. Say **a** just as you reach the end of **a**. Ask your child to repeat. Repeat Steps 1 and 2 a few times.

3   Explain that the **Flashcard** (picture side) is the same as your drawing. Tell your child that the letter is hidden behind the picture. Show the letter side. Say **a**.

4   Ask your child to say **a** or **apple** as you flip the card a few times.

Review the sounds

Once you have a number of sounds to review, hide the new sound in the pack of sounds taught so far. Ask your child to read the sounds (without bouncing or stretching them) and spot the new sound.

Use the **Bedroom Frieze** to review the sounds taught so far and any new sounds every evening. Point to the sounds your child has learnt in and out of order. Increase the speed as your child gains confidence.

Reading the digraphs with your child

A digraph is a combination of two letters used to represent one sound. When teaching the digraphs, explain to your child that the two letters are 'special friends'. Remember that each digraph is also either a stretchy (*sh*, *th*, *ng*, *nk*) or a bouncy (*ch*, *qu*) sound.

Use this plan to help your child read each digraph, e.g. *sh*. The digraphs are

Using the Flashcards

Start by holding up the **Flashcard** for *sh* (letter side). Stretch **shhhh**. Force out your lips and put your finger to your mouth.

Read the sound

1 Copy a simple version of the snake and the horse on to a piece of paper. Say the snake is making a nasty **ssss** noise and the horse tells the snake to **shhhhh**.

2 Write **sh** on the paper beside your copy of the snake and the horse. Make it the same size. Run your finger over the **sh**, saying **shhhhh**. Say **sh** as you touch the end of **sh**. Ask your child to repeat. Repeat Steps 1 and 2 a few times.

3 Tell your child that these letters are 'special friends'. Explain that the **Flashcard** (picture side) is the same as your drawing. Tell your child that the letters are hidden behind the pictures. Show the letter side. Say **shhhhh**.

4 Ask your child to say **sh** or **shhhh says the horse**, as you flip the card a few times.

Review the sounds

Hide the new sound in the pack of sounds taught so far. Ask your child to read the sounds (without bouncing or stretching them) and spot the new sound. Increase the speed as your child gains confidence.

Use the **Bedroom Frieze** to review the sounds taught so far and any new sounds every evening. Point to the sounds your child has learnt in and out of order. Increase the speed as your child gains confidence.

Handwriting

As your child is learning to read the Set 1 Speed Sounds (using the **Flashcards** and **Bedroom Frieze**), you can also teach your child to write them. As with reading, you should only refer to the sounds at this stage and not to the letter names. The **Handwriting Workbook**, together with the **Wipe-clean Sheet** and **Pen**, gives your child the opportunity to develop and practise handwriting (writing the letter or letters while saying a mnemonic phrase) and sound-writing (writing the letter or letters while saying the sound).

Although we want children to learn to write as easily as they learn to read, there are many children who, however well they can read the sounds, words and stories, find the physical process of writing more difficult. Research shows that children's intellectual progress depends on their progress in reading. This means that children who find handwriting challenging (often boys) must not be held back by this, but be allowed to progress at the speed they can learn to read. For example, if your child can read the Speed Sounds in group 1, but finds writing them challenging, they should still progress to reading and writing the group 2 sounds.

Write the letter

Use the plan below to help your child write each of the Speed Sounds as they learn to read them. You will need the **Wipe-clean Sheet** and **Pen**, the **Handwriting Workbook** and a pencil.

Example: *m*

Handwrite

Each sound in the **Handwriting Workbook** has a mnemonic (memorable phrase) to help your child learn to write that sound, for example 'Maisie, mountain, mountain'. This phrase always appears in the 'Practise handwriting' box in the **Handwriting Workbook**.

Practise handwriting

Maisie, mountain, mountain

Start by helping your child to handwrite the sound while saying the mnemonic phrase.

1 Write over **m** on the **Wipe-clean Sheet**, saying **Maisie, mountain, mountain** as you go down Maisie and then over the two mountains.

2 Wipe clean, then ask your child to do the same – writing over **m** while saying **Maisie, mountain, mountain**.

3 Ask your child to practise this until they feel confident.

Sound write

Next, help your child to write while they say the sound.

1 Write over **m** on the **Wipe-clean Sheet**, saying **m**.
2 Wipe clean, then ask your child to do the same – writing over **m** while saying **m**.
3 Ask your child to practise this until they feel confident.

> Don't worry if your child's writing is untidy.

Use the Handwriting Workbook

When your child feels confident with each sound, turn to the relevant page in the **Handwriting Workbook** and ask them to complete the writing activities.

Speed write

Once your child has learnt more than one sound, they can practise speed writing on paper or on the practice pages at the back of the **Handwriting Workbook**.

Select sounds your child has been taught so far. For example, say **mmmmm**, **a-a-a-a**, as your child writes the sounds.

> Remember to keep praising your child as they are learning to read and write. Give them specific praise for working hard.

Sound-blending

Your child will be ready to blend sounds together to read words once they have learnt the first group of sounds (***m, a, s, d, t***) and can say them in and out of order at speed.

If your child uses *Read Write Inc. Phonics* at school, they may refer to the practice of sounding out letters in words as 'Fred Talk'. Fred is a toy character that some teachers use to engage children in saying the sounds correctly.

The following pages contain activities for blending sounds together. Learning to sound-blend can take some time to master, so don't worry if your child doesn't pick it up right away. Carry on teaching your child the next group of Speed Sounds. When that group is learnt in and out of order and at speed, practise the sound-blending activities on the following pages with those sounds and the previous sounds learnt. Continue until all six groups of sounds have been learnt.

When your child can sound-blend all the groups of Speed Sounds, celebrate the success! They have reached a major milestone in learning to read.

Sound-blending 1

Step 1 **Blending orally (without the Flashcards)**

Make words with the sounds your child can read.

mat, dad, mad, sad, at, sat

If your child is using Fred Talk at school, remind them that Fred can only say the word in sounds so we have to help him. Fred says **m-a-t** and we say **mat**.

Ask your child to look at you as you:

- Say the sounds in an exaggerated manner, e.g. **m-a-t**. Ask your child to copy.
- Say the sounds followed by the whole word, e.g. **m-a-t, mat**. Ask your child to copy.

Repeat a few times, saying both the sounds and word in an exaggerated manner. Give the meaning of the word if necessary.

Step 2 **Blending with the Flashcards**

- Say **mat** clearly again. Say **I need m, a, t**. Place the cards on the table.
- Point to the sounds and say **m-a-t**. Ask your child to repeat.
- Sweep your finger under the word and say **mat**. Ask your child to repeat.

- Mix up the cards and give them to your child to make the word.
- Ask your child to point to the sounds and read the word.
- Repeat with the other words listed above – ***dad, mad, sad, at*** and ***sat***.

Reading the Green Words

The words *mat*, *dad*, *mad*, *sad*, *at* and *sat* are Green Words – words that your child will be able to read once they have learnt the Speed Sounds in this group.

Write each of these Green Words on a piece of paper. For each word:

1 Ask your child to say the sounds and read the word – without your help.

2 Repeat the word with exaggerated pronunciation and ask your child to copy.

Sound-blending 2

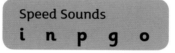

Speed Sounds

i n p g o

Review Speed Sounds

m, a, s, d, t, i, n, p, g, o

Practise reading the **Flashcards**.

Ensure your child can read these sounds quickly. Give praise for how well they read them.

Follow the blueprint instructions for teaching sound-blending on pages 16–17. Using the same method, practise these Green Words:

in, on, it, an, and, pin, got, dog, sit, tip, pan, gap, dig, top

Sound-blending 3

Review Speed Sounds

m, a, s, d, t, i, n, p, g, o, c, k, u, b

Practise reading the **Flashcards**.

Ensure your child can read these sounds quickly. Give praise for how well they read them.

Follow the blueprint instructions for teaching sound-blending on pages 16–17. Using the same method, practise these Green Words:

bin, cat, cot, can, kit, mud, up, cup, bad, ba<u>ck</u>, ki<u>ck</u>, sa<u>ck</u>, so<u>ck</u>

The underlined letters are digraphs and should be pronounced as a single sound.

18

Sound-blending 4

Review Speed Sounds

m, a, s, d, t, i, n, p, g, o, c, k, u, b, f, e, l, h, sh

Practise reading the **Flashcards**.

Ensure your child can read these sounds quickly. Give praise for how well they read them.

Follow the blueprint instructions for teaching sound-blending on pages 16–17. Using the same method, practise these Green Words:

met, set, fan, fun, fat, lip, log, let, had, hit, hen, <u>sh</u>ip, <u>sh</u>op, fi<u>sh</u>

The underlined letters are digraphs and should be pronounced as a single sound.

Sound-blending 5

Review Speed Sounds

m, a, s, d, t, i, n, p, g, o, c, k, u, b, f, e, l, h, sh, r, j, v, y, w

Practise reading the **Flashcards**.

Ensure your child can read these sounds quickly. Give praise for how well they read them.

Follow the blueprint instructions for teaching sound-blending on pages 16–17. Using the same method, practise these Green Words:

red, run, rat, jog, jet, jam, vet, yap, yes, yum, web, win, wish, wet

The underlined letters are digraphs and should be pronounced as a single sound.

20

Speed Sounds

th   z   ch   qu   x   ng   nk

Review Speed Sounds

m, a, s, d, t, i, n, p, g, o, c, k, u, b, f, e, l, h,
sh, r, j, v, y, w, th, z, ch, qu, x, ng, nk

Practise reading the **Flashcards**.

Ensure your child can read these sounds quickly. Give praise for how well they read them.

Follow the blueprint instructions for teaching sound-blending on pages 16–17. Using the same method, practise these Green Words:

<u>th</u>in, <u>th</u>ick, <u>th</u>is, zap, zip, <u>ch</u>in, <u>ch</u>op, <u>ch</u>at, <u>qu</u>iz, fox, box, fix, six, si<u>ng</u>, ba<u>ng</u>, <u>thing</u>, wi<u>nk</u>

The underlined letters are digraphs and should be pronounced as a single sound.

21

Spelling

At school, your child may be using 'Fred Fingers' to help them to spell Green Words. To use Fred Fingers with your child at home, model how you:

1   Hold up the correct number of fingers for sounds (i.e. three for **mat**).

2   Say the word, e.g. **mat**.

3   Say the sounds as you pinch each sound on to three fingers: **m-a-t**, looking at your own fingers as you do this.

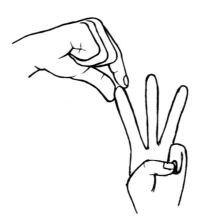

4   Ask your child to repeat.

Once you know your child can work out how many sounds there are in a word, follow this plan for each word used in the sound-blending activities.

1. Tell your child the number of fingers to hold up.

2. Say the word and ask your child to repeat and then pinch their fingers as they say the sounds.

3. Ask your child to write the word as they say the sounds. Underline any 'special friends' for them if necessary.

4. Write the word on paper and ask your child to check their spelling of each sound.

Synthetic Phonics Glossary

Read Write Inc. and synthetic phonics use vocabulary that may be unfamiliar to many parents. This glossary should familiarise you with some of the terms.

Digraph a single sound that is represented by two letters, e.g. *sh*

Green Words words that your child will be able to read once they have learnt the Speed Sounds in that word

Fred Talk saying each sound in a word

Pure sounds sounds without an intrusive *uh* at the end, *l* not *luh*, *t* not *tuh*, etc. (see page 5)

Sound-blend blending the sounds in a word together, e.g. c-a-n → can (see page 15)

Speed Sounds the letters and the sounds that words are made up of (see page 6). They are taught using the **Flashcards**.

Synthetic phonics the teaching of reading in which sounds and the letter (or letters) that represent them are pronounced individually and then blended together ('synthesised')